MONROE TOWNSHIP PUBLIC LIBRARY

BLEEDING
KANSAS

Essential Events

BLEEDING

KANSAS

BY RICHARD REECE

Content Consultant

Brie Swenson Arnold, Assistant Professor of History
Coe College

ABDO
Publishing Company

CREDITS

Published by ABDO Publishing Company, PO Box 398166,
Minneapolis, MN 55439. Copyright © 2012 by Abdo Consulting
Group, Inc. International copyrights reserved in all countries.
No part of this book may be reproduced in any form without
written permission from the publisher. The Essential Library™
is a trademark and logo of ABDO Publishing Company.

Printed in the United States of America,
North Mankato, Minnesota
102011
012012

 THIS BOOK CONTAINS AT LEAST 10% RECYCLED MATERIALS.

Editor: Lauren Coss
Copy editor: Rebecca Rowell
Cover design: Marie Tupy
Interior design and production: Kazuko Collins

Library of Congress Cataloging-in-Publication Data
Reece, Richard, 1948-
  Bleeding Kansas / by Richard Reece.
     p. cm. -- (Essential events)
  Includes bibliographical references and index.
  ISBN 978-1-61783-307-6
  1. Kansas--History--1854-1861--Juvenile literature. 2. Slavery-
-Political aspects--Kansas--History--19th century--Juvenile
literature. I. Title.
  F685.R316 2012
  978.1'02--dc23

                              2011036492

J978.102
R66

TABLE OF CONTENTS

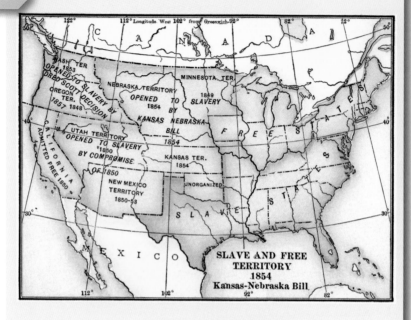

The Kansas-Nebraska Act amended the Missouri Compromise to allow territories to decide whether to permit slavery in new states.

THE KANSAS QUESTION

On March 3, 1854, the members of the US Senate had been arguing all night. In fact, they had been arguing for months. And thanks to dozens of highly opinionated newspapers across the United States, ordinary Americans were informed about their debate and had been arguing right along with them. The subject of all this discussion was the Kansas-Nebraska bill. Lawmakers were trying to decide if slavery would be allowed to expand into the new territories of Kansas and Nebraska.

In 1854, the United States had grown to extend all the way to the West Coast. California had been admitted as a state in 1850. But it had no neighboring states. The next westernmost states in the Union were Missouri and Texas. Most of the land in between was unorganized territory, not yet settled by white Americans.

The area now known as Kansas was not yet a state, but it had a few white settlers and a great deal of desirable, fertile land. Some government leaders felt it was time to officially organize Kansas as a territory, along with Nebraska to its north. That way, the US government could appoint a governor, the settlers could elect a legislature and, in time, Kansas could be admitted to the Union as a state.

This proposal was made official in the Kansas-Nebraska bill. What made the bill controversial was the question of whether slavery would be legal in the new territories. The extension of slavery was a subject on which Americans had never fully agreed.

In 1783, the young country had won its independence from Great Britain in the American Revolution. Citizens and lawmakers alike were fiercely proud of the union they had created, and early legislation focused on national unity.

A law passed in 1820, known as the Missouri Compromise, stated that black people could not be held as slaves in areas north of latitude 36°30′ north. Since Kansas was north of this latitude, the Missouri Compromise made holding slaves there illegal.

In 1820, Americans creating

The Missouri Compromise

When the Missouri Territory first petitioned for statehood in 1817, the nation was already divided over the slavery issue. At the time, there were 22 US states: 11 slave and 11 free. This translated to equal representation in the US Senate. Since slaves were already living in Missouri and Missouri had requested admission as a slave state, Southern slave states supported its admission with slavery. Those from free states, however, were concerned that the admission of another slave state would upset the political balance between free and slave states. They hoped to ban slavery in Missouri.

In 1820, the two sides reached a compromise crafted by Henry Clay, a senator from Kentucky. Clay had earned the nickname "the Great Pacificator" for his work to ease this political crisis over slavery. His efforts resulted in what became known as the Missouri Compromise. By the terms of the compromise, slavery was banned forever above latitude 36°30′ north. The exception was Missouri itself, which was above the line. As part of the compromise, Missouri was admitted as a slave state and Maine was admitted as a free state. This preserved the balance of power in the Senate.

the Missouri Compromise were willing to set aside their differences over slavery to keep the nation together. However, as the senators argued through the night in 1854, this was about to change.

Deep Divisions

The Kansas-Nebraska bill the senators were debating threatened to overturn the Missouri Compromise. Instead of following a geographic line between slave and free territory, the bill stated that each new territory would decide for itself, based on a vote by its residents, whether to be slave or free.

Democratic Senator Stephen A. Douglas of Illinois authored the Kansas-Nebraska bill. One of the most well-known statesmen of his time, Douglas's short stature and powerful presence earned him the nickname the "Little Giant." Douglas believed democracy meant

Political Parties

At the time of the Kansas-Nebraska Act, there were two main political parties: the Democratic and the Whig. The Democratic Party's members were largely proslavery. They believed in limited federal government and states' rights. They supported Douglas's push for popular sovereignty in new territories. The Whig Party had been a major player in US politics in the first half of the nineteenth century, but by the 1850s, the party was beginning to split over the issue of slavery. The presidential election of 1852 would be the last one to feature a Whig candidate. Proslavery Whigs would join the Democratic Party. Antislavery Whigs would begin forming the new Republican Party in 1854.

"The Great Pacificator," Senator Henry Clay, helped a divided Congress negotiate the Missouri Compromise.

the citizens of a state, not the federal government, should rule on important questions affecting their lives. This idea was known as popular sovereignty. In 1854, the word *people* meant white men.

Douglas underestimated how much the slavery question divided Americans. Slave owners, who supported the Kansas-Nebraska bill, pointed out that the US Constitution guaranteed the right to own property—and they considered their slaves property. Slaveholders were fearful that those who did not own slaves, particularly those in the North, would try to take this right away from them in the new western territories. Even more important, the slaveholders knew the admission of free states would reduce their political power in Congress. A long-standing balance between slave and free states had helped slavery supporters in Congress preserve the interests of slave owners. The admission of more free states, the slave owners believed, would lead to a loss in power and ultimately an end to slavery.

Other Americans opposed the bill. Some believed, many for religious reasons, that slavery was immoral and went against the values the United States had been built on. They did not want slavery anywhere in the country. They questioned how the United States could call itself the home of liberty while some of its citizens owned human beings. Many of these people became abolitionists. They worked to abolish, or end, slavery.

Another large group of Americans opposed slavery and the Kansas-Nebraska bill for economic and political reasons. If slavery was legal everywhere, they reasoned, then no one would pay free citizens for their labor.

Stephen A. Douglas

Douglas was first elected to the US Senate in 1846. He became known as both a leader and someone skilled at getting opposing parties to reach agreement on difficult issues. Douglas never saw slavery as a moral issue. Like many white Americans of his time, he considered blacks intellectually inferior to whites and incapable of ever being full citizens. Running in 1858 for his third Senate term, he was challenged unsuccessfully by a state politician named Abraham Lincoln. The two men disagreed about the extension of slavery and the place of blacks in US society. Lincoln would go on to defeat Douglas in 1860 when both men ran for president.

Douglas pushed heavily for his bill in the Senate, and on March 5, 1854, he got what he wanted. The Senate passed the bill with a 37–14 vote, making the bill the Kansas–Nebraska Act. In May, it would go to the House of Representatives.

In the House of Representatives, opponents hoped to bury the Kansas–Nebraska Act under other business, but advocates of the bill managed to bring it to the floor for debate and a vote. For a solid week, representatives passionately argued both sides. Speakers insulted each other and physical fights nearly broke out. On May 22, 1854, the House narrowly approved the bill with a 113–100 vote. President Franklin Pierce signed the Kansas–Nebraska Act into law on May 30. But the debate was far from over.

Senator Stephen A. Douglas of Illinois authored the Kansas-Nebraska bill.
He later ran for president in the election just prior to the Civil War.

As early as 1619, British colonists brought slaves to America.

Slavery in the United States

By 1619, British colonists had begun using African slaves in their Jamestown Colony in Virginia. By the late seventeenth century, nearly all North American British colonies used slavery. North America's economy was dependent on slave labor and plantation-style agriculture. Throughout the eighteenth century, the farming of tobacco, rice, and sugar in the South relied on money and supplies from the North. The goods produced by slave labor supplied factories in the North and trade with Europe. Slavery was most visible in the South, but it fueled the wealth of all the North American colonies.

After the colonies won independence from Great Britain in 1783, some US leaders tried to limit the extension of slavery. In 1787, the Northwest Ordinance banned slavery in the territories north and west of the Ohio River. By 1808, it was illegal to bring African slaves to the United States. But slaves continued to be moved, sold, and traded within the country. Slaveholding areas expanded from Virginia and the Carolinas to Mississippi and Alabama, and as far west as Texas. By 1840, there were some 2.5 million slaves in the United States. The number of slaves was not diminishing as some of the US founders had hoped.

In an effort to keep a fledgling nation together and, in many cases, to protect their own interests as slave owners, the Founding Fathers had stopped short of outlawing slavery in the US Constitution.

The third US president, Thomas Jefferson, was a slave owner who had helped draft the Declaration of Independence. He shared the feelings of many in the United States. He wondered whether slavery was at odds with a country founded on liberty, but he despaired of changing a profitable system. Even decades after the American Revolution, Jefferson simply hoped slavery would one day go away on its own. "The revolution in public opinion which this cause requires," he wrote, "is not to be expected in a day, or perhaps in an age; but time, which outlives all things, will outlive this evil also."[1]

The former president gauged public opinion accurately. Whites in the South were unwilling to do away with slavery anytime soon. They considered slavery inseparable from their own lives, liberty, and pursuit of happiness. And in the North, those who felt slavery to be immoral were a minority. Most whites in the North saw blacks as socially and intellectually inferior and would not have wanted to associate with them personally. While they were uncomfortable with slavery, they felt nothing could be done other than let time take its course. Slavery was not something people in the North often had to see with their own eyes.

BUBBLING UNREST

With the Missouri Compromise of 1820, it seemed as if the slavery question had been settled. By admitting Maine as a free state and Missouri as a slave state, congressional balance had been maintained. But the issue remained a sore point for a few vocal Americans as millions of blacks continued to live in unjust conditions.

These voices continued calling for an end to slavery. Their antislavery activities ranged from lawful protest, such as submitting

The Abolition Movement

Beginning in the late eighteenth century and continuing through the mid-nineteenth century, both whites and blacks founded dozens of abolition societies. Abolitionists were hated and scorned by many white Americans in both the North and the South. When they traveled, they were often met with harassment and violence. In 1838, an angry mob burned a Philadelphia hall to the ground while an abolitionist convention was being held in it. Most abolitionists preached nonviolence, but some would eventually advocate using force to free slaves and punish owners. They argued that violence and war might be the only way to end slavery once and for all.

In Boston, Massachusetts, white journalist and editor William Lloyd Garrison published the first issue of an antislavery newspaper called the *Liberator* in 1831. Garrison promised to be "as harsh as truth and as uncompromising as justice" in his advocacy for African-American slaves.[2] Garrison and his newspaper would become a well-known voice of the abolition movement in the United States. In 1833, Garrison and other advocates of the immediate freeing of slaves gathered in Philadelphia to form the American Anti-Slavery Society. The *Liberator* continued publication until the abolition of slavery in 1865. The American Anti-Slavery Society dissolved shortly after, in 1870.

petitions and resolutions to lawmakers and publishing and distributing pamphlets, to civil disobedience, including helping slaves escape and hide from their owners. In 1833, black and white abolitionists met in Philadelphia, Pennsylvania, and formed the American Anti-Slavery Society, which condemned slavery and called for its immediate end.

Although all abolitionists wanted to end slavery, they did not necessarily see blacks and whites as equals. Some white abolitionists protested the inhumane treatment of slaves, rather than the racial inequality associated with slavery.

Building tensions between the North and South over slavery came out in the open in the Congress of 1835–1836. A petition was submitted requesting that slavery be abolished in the District of Columbia. Such petitions had come before lawmakers many times before and been politely tabled—postponed and never debated. But this time, the slave states, led by Senator John C. Calhoun of South

Frederick Douglass

Frederick Douglass was an African-American abolitionist. In 1838, he escaped from slavery at the age of 21. Three years later, he delivered an anti-slavery speech that was so successful the Massachusetts Antislavery Society hired him as a lecturer. His autobiography of moving stories of his life as a slave in Maryland, *The Narrative of the Life of Frederick Douglass*, made him famous. After its publication in 1845, Douglass continued to be a leader in the causes of antislavery and black civil rights. Douglass later served as an adviser to President Abraham Lincoln during the Civil War.

Carolina, took action. It was time, Calhoun felt, to put a stop to these petitions and their negative reflections on the South and its people.

Calhoun was proslavery and pro-states rights. He and many other Southern politicians feared that any limitation of slavery beyond the Missouri Compromise threatened the entire institution of slave labor. The outcries of abolitionists, while relatively few in number, caused proslavery Southerners to fear for their way of life. They pictured a ruined economy, mixing of the races, and even retaliation by former slaves against their owners. A successful slave revolt in the 1790s in the French Caribbean colony of Saint Domingue (now Haiti) had resulted in bloodshed, destruction of property, and the overthrow of slavery and the rule of white slave owners. In 1831, a slave revolt in Virginia led by Nat Turner had been suppressed, but not before more than 50 whites had been killed. In the slavery debate in the United States, white Southerners' fears of slave revolts and the possibility of ending white rule triggered hysterical language. In one speech, Congressman Waddy Thompson, Jr., a representative from South Carolina, accused abolitionists of being "accessories before the fact

Nat Turner's Rebellion

In 1831, a Virginia slave rebellion created fear among many white slave owners and the slave-owning community. Nat Turner was a deeply religious slave born in Virginia in 1800. On August 21, 1831, Turner and a small band of six accomplices killed the family who owned him and started a violent revolt that lasted two days. State and federal troops eventually captured Turner and the many slaves who had joined his cause, but not before the slaves had killed at least 55 whites. Turner and more than 50 others were executed for participating in his revolt. In the violence that followed, many slaves who had not participated in the revolt were punished, harmed, or killed.

. . . of murder, robbery, rape, infanticide."[3]

Hostility between the North and the South grew alongside fears of succession. When California requested admittance to the Union as a free state in 1849, Congress attempted yet another compromise. Seventy-year-old Henry Clay, who had fashioned the Missouri Compromise, tried once again to satisfy the interests and ease the fears of both the North and South in order to maintain the Union. He proposed a series of compromises intended to appeal to both Northern and Southern politicians. These measures collectively became known as the Compromise of 1850.

The collection of compromises placed no restrictions on slavery in the new territories acquired after the Mexican-American War (1846–1848). To restrict slavery or not would be decided for each

*Nat Turner was captured and executed for his role
in leading a slave rebellion in 1831.*

new territory by the settlers who lived there. The
exception was California, which was admitted as a
free state. In the District of Columbia, slaves could
be owned but not sold or traded. To offset the
admission of California, which added a free state
without adding a new slave state, Congress passed the
Fugitive Slave Act, which required all citizens to help
in the recovery and return of runaway slaves. During
this time, many runaway slaves and even some free
blacks in the North were captured and brought to

Uncle Tom's Cabin

Harriet Beecher Stowe wrote the novel *Uncle Tom's Cabin; or, Life Among the Lowly* in response to the Fugitive Slave Act of 1850. The book, first published in 1852, portrayed Tom, a Christian slave enduring the cruelty of the vicious slave owner Simon Legree. In its first year, the novel sold 300,000 copies in the United States and 1.5 million worldwide. The book gave a bigger boost to the abolitionist cause than any previous pamphlets, newspapers, or lectures. Many white Northerners were shocked and moved by the novel's detailed portrayal of the cruelty of slavery. White Southerners were incensed. The novel had such a cultural and political impact on the national division over slavery that when Lincoln met Stowe in 1862, he supposedly said, "So you are the little woman who wrote the book that started this great war!"[4]

the South. Anyone who helped a slave escape could face heavy penalties. However, many slaves continued to run away, some aided by whites. Thousands of escaped slaves and free blacks moved to Canada during this time to avoid capture.

This compromise gave both proslavery Southerners and antislavery Northerners a victory, but the Fugitive Slave Act angered many in the North. Slavery for the typical white Northerner had always been something unpleasant but far away. Now, the law was requiring them to help enforce slavery. By the time of the Kansas-Nebraska Act in 1854, people who had been undecided about slavery were starting to feel as if they had a stake in the debate.

Harriet Beecher Stowe drew international attention to the abolitionist cause with her bestselling novel, Uncle Tom's Cabin.

*Settlers on both sides of the slavery debate staked claims
in the Kansas Territory, though the proslavery Missourians often had
no intention of actually living in Kansas.*

THE RACE TO KANSAS

In 1854, the Kansas-Nebraska Act effectively repealed the Missouri Compromise. For 34 years, that national contract had kept slavery and freedom in their respective places: South and North. The act created two new territories that were up for grabs. Antislavery advocates were outraged, and slavery supporters saw an opportunity to expand slavery further west. Under the principle of popular sovereignty, the people and lawmakers of Kansas would decide whether their state would be slave or free. Both sides saw the election of the Kansas territorial legislature as the key to winning Kansas. Whichever side could attract the most voters to Kansas to elect a legislature aligned with their view on slavery would determine the slavery status of the future state.

Missouri slave owners along the border with Kansas had an especially large stake in the debate. Nebraska was far enough north that it was likely going to become a free state, so these Missourians wanted Kansas for the proslavery side. They immediately began planning to journey into Kansas to vote in the election of the territory's legislature. Some went so far as to stake claims, pieces of land, in Kansas. Whether they planned to live there or not, they wanted to be part of the decision to come.

Missouri senator David Atchison, a Democrat, anticipated the rush to Kansas and wrote about the important role of the territory to the nation:

We are playing for a mighty stake. If we win we carry slavery to the Pacific Ocean. If we fail we lose Missouri, Arkansas and Texas and all the territories; the game must be played boldly. [1]

Charles Robinson

One of the most famous Kansas settlers of this time was Charles Robinson. He would become the spokesman for free-state emigrants in Kansas. He began as an agent for the NEEAC guiding the first party from Boston on July 17, 1854. Robinson called it "a party of twenty nine men, who were willing to take their lives in their hands." He departed "with the certainty of meeting a hostile greeting of revolvers, bowie-knives, and all the desperadoes of the border." [2]

Robinson had worked in the California gold fields in 1849 and served in the California legislature before joining the NEEAC. After settling in Kansas, he helped establish the free-state town of Lawrence. Free-soil settlers looked to him for encouragement in the face of proslavery opposition. They elected him governor under the Topeka Constitution, and he became the first legal governor of Kansas when it became a state in 1861. During those years, he was threatened countless times and arrested by the proslavery Kansas authorities. A proslavery mob burned his home in the 1856 Sack of Lawrence. His wife, Sara, was equally influential and nationally known for her free-soil activism.

Settlers from the North also wanted a say in the fate of the new territory. These emigrants, called Free-Soilers or free-staters, opposed the extension of slavery into Kansas, but most were not abolitionists. Many did not want to allow free blacks into the territory. They envisioned a free white Kansas.

Some settlers from the North did hold strong

abolitionist views. They felt that moving to Kansas to oppose slavery was a moral obligation. Proslavery Missourians did not distinguish between these groups. In their view, anyone opposed to the extension of slavery in Kansas was an abolitionist.

Between May 1854 and March 1855, the settler population of Kansas grew from fewer than 800 to more than 8,000, including 192 black slaves. Much of that migration was fueled by emigrant societies. These societies offered settlers assistance and group discounts on travel to Kansas, with the goal of promoting antislavery and free-soil settlement in Kansas. The most prominent of these societies was the New England Emigrant Aid Company (NEEAC).

Free-state settlers often arrived in family groups consisting of men, women, and children. Approximately one-third of the early settlers came

Eli Thayer and the NEEAC

Wealthy businessman Eli Thayer founded the NEEAC in Boston in 1854. Thayer marketed shares of stock in the company as a way to promote free-soil settlement of Kansas and make a statement against slavery. In 1855, the company assisted approximately 1,000 settlers in emigrating to Kansas. The NEEAC not only assisted travelers, it also built a town for them. Lawrence, Kansas, was named after the company's treasurer, Amos A. Lawrence. The NEEAC reportedly gave its settlers guns so they could protect their land claims and fight for the free-soil cause in Kansas.

*Territorial governor Andrew Reeder chose Leavenworth,
Kansas, as a temporary capital.*

from the North, while the rest came from Missouri
and the South. Still, in the months leading up to
the expected election, the ever-increasing number
of settlers from the North surprised and disturbed
proslavery Missourians.

Showdown

Shortly after the Kansas-Nebraska Act passed,
President Pierce appointed a fellow Democrat as the
territorial governor of Kansas. Andrew Reeder was
a Pennsylvania lawyer with no experience holding

public office. He supported the idea of popular sovereignty, but his stance on slavery wavered during his time in Kansas. Reeder arrived in Kansas in October 1854. His job was to choose a temporary capital, take a census, and organize the election of a territorial legislature. He chose the city of Leavenworth as the capital. Because the census would take time, he put off the election of a legislature, scheduling it for March 1855. In the meantime, he authorized the election of a territorial delegate to represent Kansas in the US Congress on November 29, 1854.

Missourians in particular were interested in where Reeder stood on the slavery issue. He immediately angered them by saying only actual residents of Kansas would be allowed to vote. Simply having staked a claim, as many on the border had done, would not count as residency.

Andrew Reeder

Andrew Reeder, the first territorial governor of Kansas, tried to keep peace between the proslavery and free-state parties. He failed, largely due to lack of support from the presidential administration that appointed him. But he is remembered as a man of principle. When a committee demanded his signature to certify bogus election results, Reeder refused. The group threatened him. If he did not sign the certificates in 15 minutes, they said, he would be hanged. "Gentlemen," Reeder replied, "I need no 15 minutes, my mind is made up, I shall hang."[3] He was spared, and his experience in Kansas turned Reeder into a steadfast free-soil supporter.

Meanwhile, proslavery gangs called border ruffians set about intimidating Kansas settlers they suspected of free-soil sympathies. Border ruffians were organized into gangs, including the Blue Lodges and Self-Defensives. Northern emigrants traveling through Missouri found themselves accosted by these gangs and interrogated about their views on slavery. In the summer of 1854, one Self-Defensive accused a Massachusetts man of abolitionism and gave him 24 lashes. Another Northern man had half of his head shaved and was told he had to leave the state.

CORRUPTION AT THE POLLS

In spite of Governor Reeder's order that Missouri residents could not vote in Kansas, Missourians were taking no chances on the territory becoming a free state. Proslavery leaders encouraged Missourians to

Native Americans

When white settlers began arriving in Kansas in the 1850s, there were thousands of Native Americans already living there. Some groups, such as the Kansas, Osage, and Pawnee, had been living there for centuries. Whites wanted land in Kansas exclusively for themselves. In some cases, they legitimately purchased land from native peoples. In many other instances, they stole land outright, sometimes under the pretext of a law or treaty. While some Native Americans in Kansas were forcibly or voluntarily removed from the territory in the 1850s, many others remained.

cross the border and vote illegally. As a result, the elections in November 1854 and March 1855 turned into election-fraud free-for-alls. For three days before the election, ferries from Missouri carried hundreds of people a day into Kansas. One Kansas settler wrote,

> *For days before the election they crowded the roads leading to the various districts, always carrying with them a liberal supply of bad whiskey. Maddened by its influence, they were ready for any dishonorable or violent course.*[4]

At the polls, proslavery mobs threatened and drove away legitimate election judges and voters perceived as free-staters. New judges, chosen by the crowds of ruffians, invited any proslavery man in attendance to vote. While little actual violence was reported, displays of guns and knives by the thugs made the threat of violence clear.

Both the November and March elections were landslide victories for the proslavery side. But the total number of votes far exceeded the number of settlers actually residing in Kansas. Governor Reeder, faced with the blatant fraud, threw out some of the most obvious illegal votes and held a special reelection. The results were no different and not

any more legitimate. Tensions over slavery in Kansas were swiftly growing out of control, and the territory would soon erupt into violence. ⌐

Border ruffians entered Kansas with intentions to cast illegal ballots and scare off would-be free-state voters.

Franklin Pierce, the fourteenth president of the United States

A Territory Divided

The bogus election results of 1854 and 1855 upset Reeder so much that he went to Washington DC to ask Pierce for troops to supervise another election—one the governor hoped would be legitimate. The president made no promises.

Meanwhile, the new legislature convened to decide the slavery question in Kansas.

Reeder believed the elected lawmakers represented the interests of Missouri rather than Kansas, but they continued to pass laws regardless of his opposition. The governor actually feared for his life. The proslavery legislators saw Reeder as clearly aligned with the free-state cause and wrote to Pierce, asking for a new governor. In the summer of 1855, they got what they wanted. The president fired Reeder.

By that time, Kansans were split over the slavery issue and, perhaps just as concerning, divided on the legitimacy of their territorial government. In August 1855, the free-state advocates held a convention in Lawrence to form their own government, pledging resistance to what they believed was an illegitimate territorial legislature.

Franklin Pierce

Franklin Pierce was the fourteenth president of the United States. He held office for one term, from 1853 to 1857. He signed the Kansas-Nebraska Act, which he strongly advocated. A native of New Hampshire, Pierce served in the US House, Senate, and military before becoming president. He was known as a doughface, which meant he was a Northerner who sympathized with the slave-owning South. Many believe Pierce's support of the Kansas-Nebraska Act helped deepen political divisions and animosities between the North and the South.

The Topeka Constitution was drafted in the newly constructed
Constitution Hall in Topeka, Kansas.

In October, the free-staters held their own
election, choosing Reeder as their territorial
delegate to Congress and 37 others as delegates to a
constitutional convention. This new, unauthorized
government was technically illegal, but members felt
they were not fairly represented in the territorial
government because it had been illegitimately
elected. At the constitutional convention, held in
Topeka, free-staters drafted a constitution under
which they hoped Kansas could be admitted to
statehood. The constitution banned slavery, but left

the issue of allowing free blacks to settle in Kansas to a later vote. Although all the free-state delegates wanted to exclude slavery from Kansas, they were not all abolitionists. But they all felt Missourians had stolen their legitimate right to a representative government. President Pierce considered the free-staters' document, known as the Topeka Constitution, to be in rebellion and threw his support behind the proslavery government.

The free-state and proslavery Kansans had reached an impasse on the issue of slavery. Any peaceful political compromise between them was failing. The conflict, fanned by fears and the press on both sides, was about to become bloody.

The Wakarusa War

In late November, an argument over land claims between free-state settler Charles Dow and proslavery settler Franklin Coleman resulted in Coleman shooting and killing Dow. Coleman fled to Missouri after the shooting. A proslavery sheriff, Samuel Jones, arrested Jacob Branson, Coleman's neighbor. Branson had witnessed the shooting, and the sheriff wanted to keep him from testifying against Coleman.

As Jones took Branson away, a group of free-staters accosted the sheriff's posse and rescued Branson, taking him to the free-state stronghold of Lawrence. Jones felt this action challenged his legal authority. He requested troops from the new Kansas governor, Wilson Shannon, in order to invade Lawrence and bring it under control. The governor agreed and called out the state militia. In the end, between 1,000 and 2,000 men rallied to Jones's cause.

Abolition Writers

In the nineteenth century, many newspapers and writers of other literature worked to influence Americans' views on slavery. New England writer John Greenleaf Whittier was read and quoted throughout the United States as the poet of abolition. Although opposed to slavery, he did not actively work toward the abolitionist cause until he was 25. He was a part of the abolition movement from 1833 to 1842. In 1833, he wrote a pamphlet calling immediate abolition "the only practicable, the only just scheme of emancipation."[1] William Lloyd Garrison published one of Whittier's poems and encouraged the writer to develop his talent.

Lydia Maria Child was another highly influential writer during the abolition. After meeting Garrison in 1831, she devoted her life to the abolitionist cause. Her best-known abolitionist work, *An Appeal in Favor of That Class of Americans Called Africans*, was published in 1833. The book was the first of its kind, detailing the history of slavery and calling for equal rights and education for blacks.

Both Whittier and Child were active in the abolitionist movement for much of their careers, editing antislavery journals in addition to writing their own works. Their popular literary writings, still read today, reached millions of Northerners in the mid-1800s, often influencing their opinions on slavery.

Proslavery advertisements calling for men to join this militia circulated throughout the territory. An ad from the *Leavenworth Herald* read,

> *Come one, come all! The laws must be executed. The outlaws, it is said, are armed to the teeth and number one thousand men. Every man should bring his rifle, ammunition, and it would be well to bring two or three days' provisions. . . . Every man to his post, and to his duty.*[2]

The gathering was planned for December 1, and on that day some 1,200 proslavery men, mostly from Missouri, assembled on the banks of the Wakarusa River near Lawrence.

Free-staters had sounded the alarm as soon as they learned of Jones's plan, and their allies began gathering to defend Lawrence. To get to Lawrence, free-staters often had to break through proslavery patrols. One such skirmish left one free-stater dead.

Wilson Shannon

Wilson Shannon was appointed territorial governor of Kansas following Reeder's removal from the post. As a Democratic congressman representing Ohio, he had voted for the Kansas-Nebraska Act. He resigned as governor at the end of the summer of 1856. Shannon described the job of governor to his successor, John Geary, as impossible. John Gihon, Geary's private secretary, wrote of Shannon, "His description of Kansas was suggestive of everything that is frightful and horrible. . . . Murder ran rampant, and the roads were everywhere strewn with the bodies of slaughtered men."[3]

Meanwhile, in Lawrence's Free State Hotel, free-state leaders negotiated with Governor Shannon while settlers outside on both sides prepared for a fight. Many in Lawrence were as eager for armed confrontation as their would-be attackers. Above all, the governor hoped to avert further bloodshed.

The governor reached an agreement with the free-staters and ordered the proslavery mob camped outside Lawrence, now numbering 2,000 men, to go home. The free-staters claimed a moral victory, while proslavery supporters in Missouri and across the South were outraged. They considered the free-staters outlaws who were prepared to defy government authority and thought they should have been punished. The Wakarusa War was never an official war, but it was the first significant confrontation in the territory. More skirmishes were to come. Senator David Atchison told the proslavery Missourians,

> The position the Lawrence people have taken is such that it would not do to make an attack on them. . . . But boys, we'll fight some time, by God![4]

MORE VIOLENCE

In January 1856, the free-staters held their own elections under the Topeka Constitution. Border ruffians did what they could to disrupt the elections. A proslavery civilian militia group known as the Kickapoo Rangers kidnapped several free-staters on the way home from the polls. A free-state militia captain named Reese Brown and several others rescued the captive voters, but the rescuers themselves were captured the next day. All were released but Brown. A mob beat him with a hatchet and took him to his home, where he bled to death on his doorstep in front of his family. The violence in Kansas was beginning to escalate.

Kansas now had two territorial governments. The federal government acknowledged the proslavery government that had been fraudulently elected. The

Beecher Bibles

As free-state Northerners moved to Kansas in 1855 and 1856, it was apparent that they would need to defend themselves against proslavery Missourians. Their friends in the North raised thousands of dollars to buy Sharps Rifles to arm free-state militias. The weapons were smuggled into Kansas in boxes labeled as books, Bibles, or other innocent supplies. One man raising funds to buy these guns and publicly endorsing the Sharps Rifle as a good tool to fight slavery was Reverend Henry Ward Beecher, brother of Harriet Beecher Stowe. He was a New England minister and social reformer who believed armed violence might be necessary in the struggle to end slavery. After an article about the rifles appeared in the *New York Tribune*, the rifles were humorously referred to as "Beecher Bibles."[5]

other government was elected more fairly and better represented Kansas citizens, but it was condemned by federal authorities. As president, Pierce issued a proclamation ordering that the outlaw, free-state government disband and threatening to send troops to suppress it.

The free-staters pledged to continue resisting the proslavery government, but without violence. Despite this pledge, as spring arrived, more settlers from the North crowded into Kansas and some brought guns. In April 1856, Sheriff Jones, who had led the militia in the Wakarusa War, went to Lawrence to arrest a free-stater. Jones was kicked out of town and returned three days later with federal troops. With the help of the troops, he arrested six free-staters who had obstructed his earlier efforts. That night, as he was camping outside town, Jones was shot in the back in his tent.

Samuel Jones

A Virginian by birth, Samuel Jones came to Kansas in 1854. He received his appointment as sheriff of Douglas County as a reward for his activities as a border ruffian. In the election of March 1855, Jones destroyed a ballot box in Bloomington, Kansas. Jones did not hesitate to use violence in the pursuit of his duties, which involved arresting free-staters he believed were in defiance of the territorial authorities. His actions made him a hero to slavery supporters and a villain to free-staters.

Although Jones was only wounded and soon recovered, local proslavery newspapers reported otherwise. "THE ABOLITIONISTS IN OPEN REBELLION – SHERIFF JONES MURDERED BY THE TRAITORS," reported the *Squatter Sovereign* of Atchison, Kansas.[6]

Within days of the shooting, the chief justice of the territory indicted the free-state leaders for treason. He ordered the free-state newspapers in Lawrence closed, as well as the Free State Hotel, which was suspected of being an arms depot and a potential fortress for free-staters.

On May 21, Jones and nearly 750 Missourians headed into Lawrence to execute the court's order. The free-staters turned over all their weapons as Jones positioned a cannon onto the town's main street. His posse bombarded and burned the Free State Hotel, burned and looted private homes, and destroyed the

Herald of Freedom

Proslavery newspapers were not alone in spreading propaganda. The *Herald of Freedom* was the voice of free-staters in Lawrence, Kansas. Founded by the NEEAC and edited by George Brown, the newspaper was also sold in New England to raise funds for the NEEAC. "If well sustained," NEEAC founder Eli Thayer advertised, it "will be one of the mightiest agencies in making Kansas a Free State."[7] The *Herald* distanced itself from violent abolitionists. Still, it was widely viewed as a paper that exaggerated, or even invented, instances of proslavery violence to influence New England readers to sympathize with the free-staters. The territorial legislature told postmasters not to distribute the *Herald* in Kansas.

printing presses of two antislavery newspapers. The only death in the violence was of a proslavery man, who was killed by a brick that fell from the crumbling hotel.

The event, known as the Sack of Lawrence, was a proslavery victory, but it reinforced support for the free-staters' cause. Just as some newspapers had misrepresented Jones's wounds, free-state propagandists exaggerated the Missourians' actions, violent language, and cries for vengeance. This increased Northern public sympathy for the free-staters in Kansas. But soon the actions of a few would destroy any lingering free-state commitment to nonviolent resistance. ⌒

The Free State Hotel in Lawrence, Kansas, was built to receive antislavery settlers. The hotel was burned to the ground in the Sack of Lawrence.

Congressman Preston Brooks assaulted Senator Charles Sumner following an antislavery speech on the Senate floor.

BLEEDING KANSAS

The conflict over slavery in the Kansas Territory was becoming known as Bloody Kansas or Bleeding Kansas. Soon, this violence would extend beyond the territory's boundaries. On May 22, 1856, one day after the Sack of Lawrence, blood was shed in the halls of Congress when another politician beat Charles Sumner, a senator from Massachusetts, with a cane.

The Caning of Charles Sumner

A few days earlier, abolitionist and Republican Charles Sumner had given a two-day speech denouncing the "Crime Against Kansas." Sumner spoke in support of a free Kansas and made personal attacks on slave-owning and proslavery senators.

In the speech, Sumner called out Democratic senators including Stephen Douglas of Illinois and Andrew Butler of South Carolina. He accused them of defending a slave system that bred humans like cattle and criticized them for trying to expand that system into Kansas. In the speech, Sumner said Butler had taken "a mistress . . . who, though ugly to others, is always lovely to him; though polluted in the sight of the world is chaste in his sight—I mean the harlot, slavery."[1] Butler was at home recuperating from a stroke and was not in attendance. Sumner went so far as to mock the speech impediment that had been one of Butler's stroke symptoms.

Butler's relative, Preston Brooks, a proslavery congressman from South Carolina, was angered

Congressional Fisticuffs

In the 1850s, as the nation approached civil war, the passions and tensions over the slavery issue often resulted in violence in Washington DC. While Brooks's caning of Sumner was an extreme example, near fistfights and duels were common in the years leading up to the Civil War. The only congressmen who were not carrying a revolver, it was said humorously, "were those carrying two revolvers."[3] In 1838, Kentucky congressman William Graves killed Maine congressman Jonathan Cilley in a duel. This prompted the House of Representatives to ban dueling within the District of Columbia.

by Sumner's insults to his relative and their home state. Three days later, Brooks found Sumner at his desk on the floor of the Senate and began beating Sumner over the head with his cane. Sumner was unable to defend himself, and other senators present, who opposed Sumner's abolitionist beliefs, waited to come to his aid. Brooks continued striking Sumner until he was unconscious and lying in a pool of blood. Sumner eventually recovered, but his injuries prevented him from returning to the Senate floor for several years.

While Northerners and free-state Kansans were outraged by the attack on Sumner, white Southerners exulted, many of them sending Brooks new canes. One was engraved, "Hit Him Again."[2] The attack made obvious the escalating regional and political divisions over slavery and Kansas. Even in the halls of the Senate, the site of so much previous political compromise over slavery, it was becoming clear that Americans were resorting to violence to resolve their differences over slavery.

THE POTTAWATOMIE MASSACRE

In Kansas, the news of Sumner's beating was the last straw for abolitionist John Brown. Like other antislavery men, Brown was coming to the conclusion that nonviolence was getting the abolition cause nowhere. For years, slave owners and proslavery supporters had used beating, lynching, and other forms of mob violence to defend their beliefs.

Brown decided it was time to retaliate with a direct attack on proslavery supporters. On the night of May 24, 1856, Brown and a small party murdered five men living near Pottawatomie Creek. Armed with guns and swords, Brown's group first went to the home of proslavery settler James Doyle and his family. When

Sara Robinson

As the turmoil in Kansas escalated, many Kansas writers tried, and were successful at, gaining Northern sympathies for the free-state movement through their works. One such writer was Sara Robinson. In 1851, she married future Kansas governor Charles Robinson. The couple was committed to a free Kansas. In 1855, Robinson followed her husband to Kansas and settled there. She was known for her free-state activism during the Bleeding Kansas years. She authored the bestselling book *Kansas: Its Interior and Exterior Life*, published in 1856, which describes in great detail the plight of free-staters in Kansas. In the book, Robinson discusses the political and social situation in Kansas, including the day-to-day violence and government corruption. The book was read by millions, earning Robinson as much fame as her husband.

Doyle answered the door, the men grabbed him and his two oldest sons, and killed all three in a nearby woods.

Brown and his men then proceeded to the cabin of proslavery attorney Allen Wilkinson, took him into the woods, and hacked him to death. Next, the gang broke into the home of James Harris. There they found William Sherman, whose family owned a tavern known to be a proslavery meeting place, and killed him. The killings became known as the Pottawatomie Massacre and made Brown a national figure. He was a demon to the South and a hero to the antislavery North.

OSAWATOMIE BROWN

Immediately after the gruesome Pottawatomie murders came to light, a proslavery militia group called Shannon's Sharp Shooters arrested two of Brown's sons, though neither had participated in the killings led by

The *New York Tribune*

Many influential voices from all over the United States took part in the debate in Kansas over slavery. Horace Greeley had established the *New York Tribune* in 1841 and was perhaps the nation's most influential journalist during the Bleeding Kansas years. The *Tribune*'s weekly national edition helped shift Northern public opinion in favor of abolition and a free Kansas. Greeley and the *Tribune* were against slavery, but not in favor of a violent approach to abolishing it. Greeley was the first to use the term *Bleeding Kansas* in his *Tribune*. He deplored the Kansas-Nebraska Act and extensively covered the conflicts in Kansas and Missouri.

John Brown's actions at Pottawatomie Creek drew attention to the ongoing struggle in Kansas.

their father. Meanwhile, Brown and his companions rode toward Osawatomie, Kansas. They had heard that Shannon's Sharp Shooters were going to attack the town and planned to be a part of its defense. Although outnumbered, Brown's group defeated the proslavery militia in a skirmish before arriving at Osawatomie.

By the summer of 1856, Brown had become something of an antislavery hero and began traveling throughout the territory around Lawrence. He met with free-staters and recruited a small group of followers he named the Kansas Regulars.

In late August, border ruffians in Leavenworth mutilated two abolitionists and shot another. Proslavery troops from Missouri were determined to stop the abolitionists. They planned an attack on Osawatomie. Brown and free-state leaders rounded up volunteers and prepared to defend the town.

On August 30, more than 300 Missourians, led by Major General John Reid, approached Osawatomie. One of the first people they encountered was Brown's son Frederick, whom they shot and killed. Then they attacked the town. Brown and the other defenders were far

John Brown

John Brown was born in Connecticut and moved throughout the east before settling in Kansas. He fathered 20 children during two marriages and worked desperately, but without much success, to support them. Brown was very religious. He involved himself in the abolition movement and devoted his life to ending slavery and helping to free blacks. Essayist and poet Ralph Waldo Emerson heard Brown speak in Boston in 1857. In his journal, Emerson wrote,

Captain John Brown of Kansas gave a good account of himself in the Town Hall, last night, to a meeting of Citizens. One of his good points was, the folly of the peace party in Kansas, who believed, that their strength lay in the greatness of their wrongs, & so discountenanced resistance. He wished to know if their wrong was greater than the negro's, & what kind of strength that gave to the negro?[4]

outnumbered. Although they inflicted damage on the Missourians, the free-staters eventually fled, and the town was burned to the ground. Brown survived but was wounded. As he watched the town burn, he told his son Jason,

> *I have only a short time to live—only one death to die, and I will die fighting for this cause. There will be no more peace in this land until slavery is done for.*[5]

Although the Missourians bragged about and exaggerated their victory, Brown's group of 38 had faced more than 200 invaders, killing between 20 and 30 and wounding approximately 40 more. But the abolitionists had still lost the town. Four free-staters were killed and three were wounded in the fighting. The Missourians captured four other free-staters and eventually killed one of them.

In the Battle of Osawatomie, John Brown was on the losing side, but he became a hero to antislavery supporters, who nicknamed him "Osawatomie Brown." He was a man who had stood for his principles against the odds and at great personal loss. Unlike those who only talked about ending slavery and keeping Kansas free, Brown fought slavery supporters with the same violence they had

used to further the proslavery cause for so long.
Some historians consider the Battle of Osawatomie
the first battle over slavery in what would become
the Civil War. As this event showed, more and
more Northerners were becoming tired of passive
resistance to the proslavery side. ⌐

John Brown

THE RIGHT MAN FOR THE RIGHT PLACE.

In a political cartoon from 1856, American Party presidential candidate Millard Fillmore, center, plays peacemaker to the two other candidates, Republican John C. Frémont, left, and Democrat James Buchanan, right.

THE PATH TOWARD STATEHOOD

In September 1856, John Geary was appointed by President Pierce to succeed Shannon as Kansas's territorial governor. Geary claimed to be completely neutral on the slavery issue and dedicated to the principle of popular sovereignty. He saw the removal of outside agitators as crucial to organizing a Kansas where the citizens could decide their own fates.

When Geary arrived in the Kansas Territory, he entered a guerilla war zone. Proslavery ruffians and free-state and abolitionist bands roamed the eastern part of the territory. At times, they fought openly, as at Osawatomie. More often, they conducted hit-and-run raids on opposing gangs or their sympathizers. One free-state man railed against "Kansas Justice," which allowed, "bands of robbers to plunder, bum, and kill."[1] President Pierce had sent federal troops to establish order, but they had been ineffective.

One of Geary's first actions, on September 15, was to break up a force of Missourians once again threatening Lawrence. When Geary personally led US troops to Lawrence, the proslavery army

A Political Shift

The Republican Party was formed in 1854 by former members of the Whig, Free-Soil, and Demo-cratic Parties to prevent the expansion of slavery by the Kansas-Nebraska Act. The party nomi-nated candidate John C. Frémont at its first presi-dential convention in 1856. In the heated cam-paign and election that followed, the Demo-cratic nominee, James Buchanan, barely edged out Frémont. Though Frémont and the Repub-licans lost, this election revealed an ominous political trend: Northern-ers and Southerners were voting almost exclusively along regional lines over the issue of slavery. It was becoming increasingly clear to the South that the North's population advantage would allow it to elect a free-soil Repub-lican candidate, who turned out to be Lincoln, in the next election.

James Lane

James Lane was a lawyer and former Democratic congressman from Indiana when he arrived in Lawrence in 1855. Lane was a man of flexible convictions regarding slavery. He was definitely not an abolitionist, but he was an opportunist, and he saw an opportunity for notoriety with the free-staters. Lane was unpolished, but he was a powerfully persuasive speaker. He became famous as a leader of the Free-State Party in Kansas and an organizer of a free-state militia against the border ruffians of Missouri. When Kansas became a state, Lane was one of its first senators. During the Civil War, Lane formed the First Kansas Colored Volunteers, one of the first black regiments to serve in the war.

surrounding the town backed off. But the fighting continued despite an order from Geary that all unauthorized militia were to disband. On September 16, 1856, free-state guerillas under the leadership of James Lane attacked a Missourian Kickapoo Ranger stronghold at Hickory Point. Lane withdrew before troops led by Geary arrived to force the disbandment of both the Missourian and free-state guerilla groups. The troops arrested scores of Lane's men and fought the Missourians until they dispersed.

Geary eased much of the violence in Kansas. But his attempt to restore popular sovereignty was discouraged at every turn by the proslavery legislature and courts of the Kansas Territory.

A Political Divide

The turmoil in Kansas was not confined to the territory.

The proslavery and free-state Kansans' failure to compromise often led to violence as they worked toward statehood.

The presidential election of 1856 revolved almost exclusively around the question of Kansas's future as a slave or free state. The election demonstrated that a political division—along a North-South boundary— over the extension of slavery was tearing the country apart. Old political parties such as the Whig collapsed and new ones such as the Republican emerged under the weight of the slavery issue. In the election of 1856, three political parties were represented in the presidential race: the Democratic, the Republican, and the American. Each hoped its candidate would win the White House.

Each party also had to take a stance on the Kansas issue. The Democrats supported the possible extension of slavery into Kansas. The Americans generally opposed the extension of slavery into Kansas. The Republicans strongly opposed the extension of slavery into Kansas and called for free soil in all new territories.

The Dred Scott Decision

As Kansans struggled to agree on a constitution, a Supreme Court ruling in 1857 led to increased support for free-soil politicians such as Abraham Lincoln. Dred Scott was a Missouri slave whose master had taken him in 1834 into free territory north of the state and then returned him to Missouri. Scott sued for his freedom, arguing that slavery was prohibited in the territory where he had temporarily lived. Lower courts had disagreed on his status, and the case, *Dred Scott v. Sanford,* made it to the Supreme Court in 1856.

The majority of the court ruled that since Scott was black and a slave he was not, and could never be, a citizen. Scott was property and, therefore, could not sue in court. Furthermore, the laws of the state where the lawsuit was brought would determine his status as slave or free. Scott had brought the lawsuit in Missouri, which ruled him still a slave. Finally, the court decided the states, not the federal government, had the right to determine whether slavery was legal or illegal within their boundaries. By this reasoning, the Missouri Compromise was unconstitutional.

Slavery supporters were triumphant. Anti-slavery Americans, and even those who were only opposed to the extension of slavery, were outraged by the decision.

Luckily for the South, Democrat James Buchanan was elected president in 1856. During the years since the Kansas-Nebraska Act, Buchanan had been the US ambassador to Great Britain, so he had no position on record in regard to the turmoil in Kansas. Also, Buchanan was a Northerner from Pennsylvania widely known to be sympathetic to the South and to slavery. On slavery in Kansas, Buchanan supported the concept of popular sovereignty. He believed it was his duty to support the outcome of the elections in the territory, even if the results favored slavery and were of questionable fairness. He simply wanted the pro-, and antislavery sides in Kansas to get along, obey the law, and "slide gracefully into the Union."[2]

A crucial step in applying for statehood was the framing of a state constitution, which had to be accepted by the US Congress and ratified by the people of the territory. In 1857, the legislature passed a bill to call a constitutional convention in the town of Lecompton, Kansas, in September. Geary vetoed the bill because there were no plans to submit the constitution to a free vote by the people of Kansas. The lawmakers passed the bill anyway. Soon afterward, the governor resigned.

A Change in Political Climate

President Buchanan appointed Democrat Robert Walker to take Geary's place as governor. Walker was sworn in on May 9, 1857. Walker was instructed to expedite the framing of a constitution that would be acceptable to both the people of Kansas and the US Congress. All the delegates elected to the constitutional convention were proslavery because the free-staters had decided to boycott the June election of delegates.

The proslavery Lecompton delegates met in September and created a constitution to be submitted to Congress. On October 6, another election was held in Topeka, the territory's temporary capital, to name representatives to the territorial legislature. Walker's efforts to keep these elections fair resulted in a free-state majority. Kansas now had a free-state legislature and a proslavery constitution.

Submitting the constitution to Congress required ratification by the citizens of Kansas, most of whom clearly did not want slavery in Kansas. To make it more acceptable to the citizens, the delegates put the constitution forward with what they called a compromise. Voters would have the choice of accepting the Lecompton Constitution with or

*Constitution Hall in Lecompton, Kansas,
the drafting site of the Lecompton Constitution*

without slavery. However, while the no-slavery option
prohibited further importation of slaves into Kansas,
it still stated, "the right of property in slaves now
in this Territory shall in no manner be interfered
with."[3] For free-staters, any degree of slavery in
Kansas was unacceptable. The choice was not a choice
at all.

Governor Walker went to Washington to tell
the president the proposed constitution in either

form did not express the wishes of
the voters in Kansas. But Southern
slavery proponents had powerfully
pressured Buchanan, so he was
eager for Congress to accept the
Lecompton Constitution. Walker
resigned.

VOTING ON LECOMPTON

The vote on December 24 to
determine whether the constitution
would be submitted with or without
slavery was as unfair as any up to that
time, and it was largely boycotted
by free-staters. The result was very
lopsided: 6,000 to 600 in favor of
the Lecompton Constitution with
slavery. Everyone in Kansas and in
Washington knew this constitution
did not reflect the wishes of the
majority of Kansans. But by the time
Congress recessed for Christmas,
it was facing the certainty that the
Lecompton Constitution would be
submitted for approval.

A Tough Job

During Kansas's territorial
period, from 1854 to
1861, Kansas had ten
different men serving as
governor or acting gov-
ernor. This added up to
a total of 25 separate
gubernatorial stints. The
shortest term was less than
20 days, and no governor
sat a full year in a single
term. The most frequent
governor was Kansas's
first secretary, Daniel
Woodson, who, though
never actually sworn in,
served as acting governor
five separate times dur-
ing Kansas's tumultuous
Bleeding Kansas years.
US territorial governors
were appointed by the US
president.

On January 4, 1858, elections were held in Kansas to determine state officers and ratify the Lecompton Constitution. Because these elections were held as required by the proslavery Lecompton Constitution, free-staters argued about whether to participate. In the end, they did, and despite proslavery attempts to tamper with the balloting, the free-staters won. The same day, Kansas's residents voted on the Lecompton Constitution itself and roundly rejected it.

Buchanan was by then committed to continuing to support his proslavery friends. He was under the illusion that accepting the proposed constitution would lead to statehood and peace in Kansas. Despite the constitution's rejection by Kansas's voters, Buchanan used all the influence and political power at his disposal to force the Lecompton Constitution through Congress.

Several issues faced the senators and congressmen in their debate on the Kansas constitution. Proslavery Southerners clashed with antislavery Northerners. For Democrats, who included most of the South and some of the North, the president had made approving the proposed constitution a test of party loyalty. For those who believed in popular

James Buchanan

The fifteenth president of the United States was a veteran, though not always savvy, politician. Age 64 when he was elected, Buchanan had been a Democratic state legislator, congressman, cabinet member under James Polk, and ambassador to Great Britain. Buchanan was a hesitant and indecisive politician. His obsession with getting Congress to approve the questionable Lecompton Constitution while Kansas and the entire United States threatened to erupt in to war was a prime example of this.

sovereignty, the document was a lie. It did not reflect the views or wishes of the majority of people in Kansas. Even Senator Stephen Douglas, the author of the Kansas-Nebraska Act, broke with Buchanan, saying,

> *I have no fear of any party associations being severed . . . I can not act with you and preserve my faith and my honor, I will stand on the great principle of Popular Sovereignty . . .*[4]

The Kansas Territory and the nation as a whole were coming apart at the seams. ⌣

James Buchanan, the fifteenth president of the United States

Charles Hamilton and his men murdered five and wounded five free-staters in a massacre along the Marais des Cygnes River in 1858.

GUERILLA WARFARE

While the Lecompton Constitution was being debated in Congress, the Kansas free-state legislature, anticipating either the constitution's defeat in Congress or its rejection by Kansans, had initiated yet another constitutional

convention, this time in Leavenworth, Kansas.
The free-state legislature's objective was to have an
alternate document to present to Congress. But
this constitution opened the possibility of giving
free blacks the right to vote. That was too much for
many of the free-staters, who wanted the territory
to be free of slavery but also free of blacks. The
proposed constitution was presented in Washington
in an unsuccessful attempt to derail debate on the
constitution approved in Lecompton.

In the end, Congress failed to pass either
constitution, but tried to sway Kansans into
accepting the Lecompton Constitution by
resubmitting it to the territory's voters and attaching
a land grant to its approval. Kansans were not
impressed. On August 2, 1858, they rejected the
Lecompton Constitution once and for all. Statehood
for the Kansas Territory remained on hold.

More Bloodshed

With Congress's continual failure to pass the
Lecompton Constitution, the free-state forces
were gaining political ground. Nevertheless, a few
extreme free-state and proslavery forces continued
to fight. Free-state and proslavery towns sat within

miles of each other, and bands of riders terrorized both sides, looting stores and businesses, stealing livestock, and assaulting and occasionally murdering settlers. One Kansas minister claimed to be averaging four funerals a week.

The most feared free-state band was called the Jayhawkers and was led by a former minister, James Montgomery. The Jayhawkers plundered proslavery settlements in southern Kansas. Their aim was driving those settlers out of the territory. In February, and again in April 1858, they fought federal troops charged with keeping order at Fort Scott, killing one of the soldiers in the skirmish.

Some proslavery settlers fought back. Charles Hamilton had come from Missouri and settled in Kansas in 1856. He fought for slavery in the territory. When his homestead was attacked by Montgomery's band in May 1858, he fled to his former state. In Missouri, he gathered a group of approximately 30 supporters to counterattack the Jayhawkers, claiming, "We are coming up there to kill snakes."[1]

The Marais des Cygnes Massacre

Back in Kansas, Hamilton's proslavery guerilla group began taking prisoners along the Marais

des Cygnes River on May 19, 1858. He marched
11 of them into a gully and ordered them to line
up. Hamilton ordered his men to fire on the
free-staters, killing five and leaving five seriously
wounded. Only one man escaped unharmed—he
pretended to be dead.

The massacre terrified settlers on both sides
of the slavery debate, and they fled the area. To
free-staters, the
murders called
for vengeance.
The free-state
Jayhawkers attacked
Hamilton's men,
wounding two.
Montgomery
followed Hamilton
into Missouri and
then convinced a
Missouri sheriff
to arrest three of
Hamilton's men
for participating in
the massacre.

Lincoln-Douglas Debates

In 1858, Abraham Lincoln and Stephen Douglas were both candidates for the US Senate from Illinois. They held a series of seven debates at various locations throughout the state. Though it was a state-level election, the main subject of the debates—slavery—made the race interesting to the entire country.

Douglas tried to stand by popular sovereignty and his Kansas-Nebraska Act. But that was not enough to satisfy many Democrats in the North who were uncomfortable about the possibility of expanding slavery into Kansas. Lincoln, while strongly advocating an end to slavery's extension, did not support abolition. He called popular sovereignty a "living, creeping lie," claiming that Kansas was not unique, but a symptom of the turmoil affecting the entire nation.[2]

Douglas, the incumbent, retained his Senate seat in the election. But his unclear stance on the expansion of slavery would turn voters in the North and the South against him in the 1860 election for president.

In December 1858, the Jayhawkers again attacked Fort Scott, freeing an imprisoned colleague, capturing townspeople, and stealing property. One resident was killed. It was reported that Montgomery bragged that he had "whipped Uncle Sam, and could do it again."[3]

John Brown also decided that the killings at Marais des Cygnes required a response. He bided his time almost until Christmas 1858. In December, he rode with 20 men into Missouri, forcibly liberated ten slaves from two different families and took them to Kansas. The governor of Missouri offered $3,000 for Brown's capture, but once across the border, Brown was safe. Just as slave owners in Missouri had feared, Kansas abolitionists were helping slaves escape and giving them sanctuary.

Brown echoed the tenuous situation when he told a news correspondent in January 1859, "The war is not over. It is a treacherous lull before the storm. We are on the eve of one of the greatest wars in history."[4]

While Kansas hoped for peace and statehood at last, the nation was coming apart as tensions between those for and against the extension of slavery approached a breaking point. In 1859, Brown did his part to accelerate events.

Brown had long dreamed of ending slavery by leading an armed slave rebellion. He had set his sights on the federal arsenal at Harper's Ferry, Virginia. In October 1859, Brown and 21 men, including five free blacks, captured the arsenal and a nearby rifle factory and arrested 60 slaveholding citizens.

Brown had believed that once their masters were captured, slaves would join his rebellion, which would then spread across the South. He was wrong. No slaves joined Brown, perhaps because no word of the rebellion had been spread to slaves in advance, there were relatively few slaves in this area, and the mission was dangerous.

Instead, the US Army, under the command of Colonel Robert E. Lee, seriously wounded Brown and killed eight of his men. Brown was captured, tried, and executed for treason on December 2, 1859.

Informing the Country

Journalists and their newspapers often tried to influence Northern opinion on Bleeding Kansas by writing on what was happening in the territory. One such journalist was James Redpath, a confirmed abolitionist who thrilled US readers with his on-site reports from the Kansas-Missouri border. "In this region," he wrote, "when men went out to plow they always took their rifles with them. . . ."[5]

Redpath's biography of Brown would do much to create the legend of a martyr to the cause of freedom for slaves. The biography also convinced many white Northerners of the acceptability of violence in that cause.

Brown's trial and execution further polarized
the country. He became a martyr to antislavery
Northerners, and despite Brown's execution, that
reaction further convinced the unhappy South that
the North was its enemy. The political tensions
between the North and South would soon boil over
into secession and war.

*John Brown's raid on Harper's Ferry was his last physical stand
against slavery.*

*The American Civil War between the Northern Union
and the Southern Confederacy lasted from 1861 to 1865.*

CIVIL WAR

When one of Kansas's many territorial governors, James Denver, retired in October 1858 after serving less than a year, guests at his farewell dinner had toasted, "'Bleeding Kansas'—The country may rest in quiet, her wounds are healed. The great question is now at rest."[1] One Kansan wrote to a friend at the end of that same year, "We are waiting anxiously to get into the Union before it *Busts*."[2]

Despite the largely unpunished violence that took place along the border throughout 1858, even Missourians could see that sooner or later Kansas would be admitted as a free state. In July 1859, a fourth constitutional convention assembled at Wyandotte (now part of Kansas City, Kansas). The document the attendees created, and which Kansas voters ratified in October, went beyond banning slavery to consider the rights of blacks. It gave both women and African Americans the right to vote in school elections and left open the possibility of full voting rights for black men.

In February 1860, Kansas's request for statehood under the Wyandotte Constitution came before Congress. The bid was accepted by the House, but continually pushed aside in the Senate.

In November, Abraham Lincoln was elected president. Proslavery Southerners saw that most Northerners and the new president opposed the extension of slavery, and Southern states now lacked the political power to protect their proslavery interests.

On December 20, South Carolina voted to secede from the Union. As the other Southern states that would make up the Confederacy continued to secede, proslavery power in Congress was greatly diminished. Kansas got the votes it needed and was finally admitted to the Union as a free state on January 29, 1861. By April, secession had led to war and Kansas joined the Union forces against the Confederacy.

Those who had been prominent warriors in Bleeding Kansas now lined up against each other in the national war. James Lane was now one of Kansas's two US senators. During the Civil War, he commanded Lane's Brigade, which consisted of the First, Third, Fourth, and Fifth Kansas Volunteers. The First Kansas Colored Volunteers would become the first regiment of black troops to see action in the war. James Montgomery was made a colonel in the Third Kansas Volunteer Brigade.

On the proslavery side, David Atchison, the former Missouri senator and encourager of border ruffians, was appointed a general in the Missouri State Guard. Missourians were divided over whether to stay in the Union or join the Confederacy. Their governor and the state legislature wanted to join the Confederacy. A convention was called to determine whether Missouri would fight for the Union or Confederate side. In spite of Missouri's proslavery ties, the convention voted to remain in the Union.

BORDER WARS

During the Civil War, while Confederate troops battled with Union troops in other parts of the country, independent groups attacked both sides along the Kansas-Missouri border according to their sympathies. The proslavery groups were sometimes known as Bushwhackers. The antislavery groups were called Jayhawkers. Both were effective and feared. A reporter for the *New York Times* wrote about the situation in 1861:

> It is beginning to be understood that a ragged fellow in the brush, with a double-barreled shotgun . . . is nearly as formidable as a Federal on a

Violence in Missouri

When the Missouri convention called to decide on secession voted to remain in the Union, a Pro-Union US military captain, Nathaniel Lyon, took all the weapons and ammunition in the state arsenal to Illinois. With this advantage, he forced the secessionists occupying Camp Jackson in Saint Louis to surrender, securing that part of Missouri for the Union.

Proslavery mobs rioted in the streets, and when one of them shot at Lyon's soldiers, he ordered his army to return fire. In the battle that followed, 28 civilians were killed.

Lyon had no regrets. "Better, sir, far better," he said to Missouri's proslavery governor, "that the blood of every man, woman and child within the limits of the state should flow, than that she should defy the federal government."[3]

prancingsteed, dressed in costly blue and armed with heavy sabre, with pistol and carbine. . . . [These men] always avoiding a direct fight, laying ambuscades where they can do the most damage with the least danger . . . are foemen much to be feared.[4]

A name that would become famous in the Civil War was William Clarke Quantrill. A Northerner, a racist, and a petty criminal, Quantrill sided with the South. He would become one of the most feared and ruthless Confederate guerillas in Missouri and Kansas.

For some who had fought through Bleeding Kansas, the Civil War was a chance for payback against the other side with the excuse of fighting for the Union or the Confederacy. Major General Henry Halleck, commander of the Union's Missouri Department, despised the pro-Union guerilla Jayhawkers. "They wear the uniform

"Bloody Bill" Anderson

William T. Anderson, known as Bloody Bill, moved to Kansas from Missouri in the late 1850s. He acquired a reputation as a horse thief and a violent man. In 1862, he had to flee Kansas to avoid being arrested for murder. He fled to Missouri, where he participated with Quantrill in the destruction of Lawrence. Then Anderson started his own gang. He and his men became known for the savagery of their attacks, not simply killing their victims, but scalping, skinning, or sometimes beheading the bodies. Anderson's gang murdered 22 Union soldiers in a train robbery in Centralia, Missouri, in September 1864. One month later, federal troops caught up with Anderson and killed the outlaw.

of . . . the United States," he wrote. "[But] their principal occupation . . . seems to have been the stealing of negroes, the robbing of houses and the burning of barns, grain and forage."[5]

There was no law, only force, to stop guerilla groups on either side from killing, looting, and terrorizing. In a typical Jayhawker raid on Osceola, Missouri, which took place on September 22, 1861, the Kansans loaded up wagons with stolen store goods, then set the town on fire. Nine people died.

A much more serious attack occurred on August 21, 1863, when Quantrill led a raid on Lawrence, which was still a symbol of abolitionism to many Missourians. The attackers targeted blacks and whites known to be antislavery. Quantrill's men killed approximately 200 men and boys and burned the town to ashes.

Jesse and Frank James

Desperate times in Bleeding Kansas spawned more than one desperate man. Perhaps the most famous was Jesse James. His family was slave-owning farmers in western Missouri. When the Civil War broke out, Jesse's older brother Frank served for the Confederacy until he was captured by Union forces and later released. Although it violated his parole, Frank joined Quantrill's Missouri Bushwhackers. After the war, Jesse and Frank and other Missouri guerillas formed a violent robbery gang that terrorized the Midwest. Jesse would blame much of his violence on his hatred of the North and his belief that the South should have won the Civil War.

In August 1863, Confederate Quantrill attacked Lawrence, Kansas, killing 200 antislavery supporters and burning the town.

In response, 3,500 Kansas men led by Lane assembled to invade Missouri. Although authorities convinced them not to carry out their revenge, Union General Thomas Ewing issued Order No. 11, requiring the evacuation of all civilians in four border counties of Missouri. The order was partly for their protection from angry Kansans and partly to move any supporters of Missouri guerillas away from the border. This order left thousands of

Missourians temporarily homeless. It also failed to stop Quantrill, who attacked Union troops just a few months later, killing 70 soldiers and 10 civilians.

In 1864, Sterling Price, a former Missouri governor and a Confederate general, led 12,000 troops into Missouri in a final effort to win the state for the Confederacy. Aided by thousands more proslavery guerillas, Price moved through southern Missouri and threatened Kansas before Union troops finally organized an

The End of the Civil War and Slavery

In March 1861, when President Lincoln gave his inaugural address, he promised the country he was not intending to end slavery. In spite of this assurance, Southern states continued to secede and the Civil War began that April. As the war raged on, Lincoln began to see emancipation as necessary to ending the war and preserving the unity of the country. In January 1863, he officially issued the Emancipation Proclamation, freeing all slaves in Confederate states.

On April 9, 1865, Confederate General Lee surrendered to Union General Ulysses S. Grant at Appomattox Court House. Lincoln would not live to see his country reunited. Just days after Lee's surrender, the president was assassinated. The remaining Confederate troops surrendered in the following weeks. On December 6, 1865, the Thirteenth Amendment passed, abolishing slavery once and for all on US soil. The Civil War was over at last, but approximately 620,000 Americans had been killed from both sides in the war years, with thousands more wounded.

The destruction in the South was devastating, and political and physical reconstruction would continue for years after the war had ended. Even though they were now free, African Americans would continue their fight for equal rights well into the twentieth century.

effective defense. By November, Union forces aided by Kansas state militia drove Price and his men back to Arkansas.

When the Civil War ended in 1865, the border violence ended as well. The Emancipation Proclamation of 1863 had freed all African-American slaves and the Thirteenth Amendment officially abolishing slavery was ratified on December 6, 1865. Kansas's black population, which was only 627 in 1860, swelled, reaching more than 17,000 by 1870. Although Kansas had stopped bleeding and former slaves were free all over the United States, many blacks continued to think fondly of the state as an early enemy of slavery. It was a place where whites such as Brown had stood up for African-American rights. ⌐

*The Emancipation Proclamation of 1863
freed all slaves in Confederate states.*

Free African-American settlers, known as exodusters, established the black community of Nicodemus, Kansas.

BLEEDING KANSAS LEGACY

leeding Kansas remains a topic of debate for some historians. Some believe it led to the Civil War, but others see it as a local problem mirroring the tensions that eventually divided the nation. What is certain is that Bleeding Kansas left a legacy. The years of violence in Kansas spurred important changes that affected the whole United States.

NEWSPAPERS

Another certainty is that the rise of newspapers in the United States made it possible for citizens throughout the country to follow the daily twists and turns of a bloody conflict taking place on their own soil. Historian Edward Ayers goes so far as to say, "Print shaped everything we associate with the coming of the Civil War."[1] The very term *Bleeding Kansas* was invented by publisher and journalist Horace Greeley and popularized through his newspaper, the *New York Tribune*.

In the nineteenth century, newspapers had very definite points of view. Most of them were not above exaggerating the truth or even making things up to entertain their readers, shape their opinions, and

Nicodemus, Kansas

When the exodusters arrived in Kansas and states farther west, they discovered that racial prejudice was not unique to the South. Some exodusters established their own all-black communities, hoping to preserve their economic autonomy and religious and family values without white oppression. The last surviving black community from this era is Nicodemus, Kansas, established in 1877 by freed slaves from Kentucky and Tennessee. At one point, the town flourished with three groceries, four general stores, two liveries, two barber shops, and four hotels. As of the 2000 census, just over 50 people resided in Nicodemus.

persuade them to act. People of the time understood the importance of newspapers. Destroying the printing presses of enemies was a common act of war, as when proslavery forces destroyed the offices and presses of free-state newspapers in Lawrence.

When the Kansas-Nebraska Act became law in 1854, and in the Bleeding Kansas years that followed, the nation was obsessed with Kansas. The views, aligned with the North and the South, were expressed in influential newspapers such as the *New York Tribune* and the *Richmond Enquirer*. Abolitionists had William Lloyd Garrison's *Liberator* in Boston and the *Herald of Freedom* in Lawrence. Proslavery factions in Missouri had the *Squatter Sovereign* and the *Kansas City Enterprise*. Bleeding Kansas taught the nation the power of the press, and the influence of media has been growing ever since.

The Rotary Printing Press

The events on the Kansas-Missouri border became Bleeding Kansas in the minds of Americans when they read about them in the newspaper. The explosion of newspapers became possible because of the rotary printing press, which was invented by Richard M. Hoe of New York in 1847. The press had lead type fastened around a cylinder that could be turned repeatedly in one direction. Then the cylinder was powered with a steam engine. Hoe's press, capable of printing 8,000 sheets an hour, was called the "lightning press."[2]

*William Lloyd Garrison published
the abolitionist newspaper the* Liberator.

John Brown

Kansas also brought John Brown before a fascinated public—not just the man, but also his conviction that violence was justified to free the slaves. Some still see Brown as a violent—even insane—fanatic, but his actions, which had been dramatized in newspapers, gained followers and played a part in tipping the balance against slavery in Kansas and the nation.

Whether Brown actually helped cause the Civil War or not is debatable. But he saw and described what many Americans at the time wanted to ignore: the institution of slavery might only be eliminated by violence and war, not through political compromise.

Sojourner Truth

When the Civil War ended, abolitionist Sojourner Truth tried unsuccessfully to find congressional support and sponsors for a black state in the West. Yet, in her eighties, she became a strong supporter of the exoduster migration from the South to Kansas. She even traveled to Kansas in the last years of her life to show her solidarity with them.

Truth was born into slavery in New York in 1797. When slaves were emancipated in New York in 1827, she found work as a household servant. She underwent a religious conversion and in 1843, became a traveling preacher. In the late 1840s, she became a popular abolitionist speaker, though she was clear about ending slavery by peaceful means.

Truth continued her speaking career—she called it preaching—during and after the Civil War. She was heavily involved in the women's suffrage movement, speaking about the rights of women as well as blacks. Whenever she spoke, she also sang, and her tall, gaunt figure and deep voice made a strong impression on those who saw and heard her. Harriet Beecher Stowe, the author of *Uncle Tom's Cabin*, met Truth and wrote in 1863, "I do not recollect ever to have been conversant with anyone who had more of that silent and subtle power which we call personal presence than this woman."[3]

Sojourner Truth

Black Rights

The violence in Kansas also had the effect of changing how some white people viewed blacks. Most settlers from the North had come to the Kansas

Territory hoping to create a free white state. The Wyandotte Constitution passed in 1859, with its guarantee of some black rights, would likely not have been accepted by a majority of Kansas's voters before the Bleeding Kansas years.

The migration of blacks from the South to Kansas rose sharply after 1877, when federal troops stationed in the South during Reconstruction returned to the North. Kansas's reputation for supporting some black rights lured many to the state in the years after the Civil War in what was called the Kansas Exodus. In 1879–1880 alone, approximately 6,000 blacks, who were known as exodusters, settled in Kansas. However, the exodusters still faced hardships in their new home. Racism existed there, the climate could be harsh, and farms were small and did not support the crops the migrants were accustomed to growing. But many still felt life in Kansas was better than life in the South.

Kansas Turns 150

Kansas celebrated 150 years, or its sesquicentennial, of statehood in 2011. In February of that year, a program about Bleeding Kansas was held in Lecompton. The US Senate passed a resolution celebrating the anniversary, and Kansas senator Pat Roberts spoke about his state. "Our state's motto, 'To the Stars through difficulty,' remains true to Kansas 150 years since its founding. We fought wars, settled the unyielding prairie, prospered in aviation and agriculture, and raised heroes that went on to lead our nation. The next 150 years hold even greater promise than that fateful day in January in 1861 when Kansas was founded based on the ideals of personal freedom and individual liberty."[4]

2011

1861 **Kansas**

USA FOREVER

A commemorative stamp celebrated the 150th anniversary of Kansas's statehood.

POPULAR SOVEREIGNTY AND POLITICAL FAILURE

Kansas was also a testing ground for popular sovereignty. While the concept seemed reasonable on the surface, its application in Kansas led to chaos and bloodshed. As Lincoln explained in his Peoria, Illinois, address in 1854, governments could not make a law extending something most people felt was morally wrong and expect a harmonious outcome. Slavery was based on the idea that one man could do whatever he wanted to another man, a principle most Americans did not agree with.

Bleeding Kansas also demonstrated that the US political system was imperfect. Compromise had failed to bring together those opposing the extension of slavery and those for it. The political process broke down, and the result was violence—both in Kansas and the United States as a whole.

However, because of this violence, some major shifts did occur for the betterment of the nation. After nearly 250 years, slavery was abolished in the United States with the Thirteenth Amendment to the Constitution in 1865. In 1868, the Fourteenth Amendment granted citizenship to African Americans and all people born in the United States. The Fifteenth Amendment, passed in 1870, granted black men the right to vote. Bleeding Kansas proved that, as Lincoln famously said in a speech at the Republican state convention, "A house divided against itself cannot stand."[5] The Bleeding Kansas years led to more rights for blacks. Americans who took part in future movements, including the civil rights movement of the 1950s and 1960s, were able to adopt more peaceful methods to bring about social and political change.

Today, the Kansas state capitol lies in Topeka. Issues are solved using peaceful political compromise, rather than the violence of Bleeding Kansas.

TIMELINE

1854	1854
On March 5, the Senate passes the Kansas Nebraska Act.	On May 22, the House passes the Kansas-Nebraska Act. President Franklin Pierce signs it into law on May 30.

1855	1856	1856
On December 1, proslavery Missourians threaten to attack Lawrence. The incident is known as the Wakarusa War.	During the Sack of Lawrence on May 21, some 750 proslavery partisans invade Lawrence, destroying its hotel and two newspaper offices.	On May 24, in an incident known as the Pottawatomie Massacre, a gang led by John Brown murders five proslavery advocates.

1854

The first New England emigrants arrive in Lawrence, Kansas, in August.

1854

The first territorial election is held in Kansas on November 29.

1855

After being shut out of the second government election in March, free-state Kansans establish their own legislature.

1856

Proslavery Missourians attack and demolish Brown's home base of Osawatomie, Kansas, on August 30.

1856

On September 15, territorial proslavery militia place Lawrence under siege. Governor John Geary disbands the militia.

1857

In September, the proslavery delegates frame a constitution in Lecompton, Kansas.

TIMELINE

1857	1857	1858
The Free-Soil Party elects a majority to the territorial Kansas legislature on October 6.	On December 24, proslavery voters approve the Lecompton Constitution with slavery for submission to Congress.	On January 4, in a second election with free-state voters participating, the Lecompton Constitution is rejected.

1860	1861	1861
On December 20, South Carolina becomes the first of 11 proslavery Southern states to vote to secede from the Union.	On January 29, Kansas is admitted to the Union as a free state.	On September 22, Jayhawkers loot and burn the town of Osceola, Missouri, executing nine of its citizens.

1858

Proslavery and
abolitionist forces
clash near the
Marais des Cygnes
River on May 19.
Missourians execute
five free-staters.

1858

Kansas's voters reject
the Lecompton
Constitution
on August 2
for the final time.

1859

The Kansas
legislature passes the
antislavery Wyandotte
Constitution in July.

1863

William Quantrill
leads a surprise
attack on Lawrence
on August 21,
sacking the city
and killing more
than 180 people.

1865

On April 9,
Confederate General
Robert E. Lee
surrenders to Union
General Ulysses S.
Grant, officially
ending the Civil War.

1865

The Thirteenth
Amendment to the
US Constitution,
officially abolishing
slavery in the United
States, is ratified
on December 6.

ESSENTIAL FACTS

DATE OF EVENT

March 5, 1854–December 6, 1865

PLACE OF EVENT

The Kansas Territory

KEY PLAYERS

❖ John Brown

❖ James Buchanan

❖ Stephen A. Douglas

❖ John Geary

❖ Franklin Pierce

❖ Andrew Reeder

❖ Robert Walker

HIGHLIGHTS OF EVENT

❖ The signing of the Kansas-Nebraska Act in 1854 repealed the Missouri Compromise, installing in its place popular sovereignty.

❖ Settlers flooded Kansas, many intending to influence whether Kansas would become a free or slave state. At first, most of the settlers were proslavery, from the neighboring slave state of Missouri, and did not actually intend to reside in Kansas.

❖ In 1856, violence broke out. Proslavery forces invaded and sacked the town of Lawrence. In Washington DC, an antislavery Northern senator was nearly killed by a proslavery Southern congressman on the floor of the US Senate. John Brown led a band of abolitionists who murdered five proslavery men. Proslavery supporters retaliated by destroying the town of Osawatomie, Kansas.

❖ Following the election of Abraham Lincoln as president in 1860, Southern states began to secede from the Union. Without proslavery opposition, Kansas joined the Union as a free state on January 29, 1861.

❖ In April 1861, the American Civil War began. In Kansas and Missouri, the guerilla warfare became more brutal. The single bloodiest incident occurred on August 21, 1863, when proslavery guerillas led by William Quantrill attacked Lawrence, burning the town and killing approximately 200 of its citizens.

❖ Hostilities along the Kansas-Missouri border ended with the surrender of the Confederacy in April 1865.

❖ Slavery was officially abolished on December 6, 1865.

Quote

"We are playing for a mighty stake. If we win we carry slavery to the Pacific Ocean. If we fail we lose Missouri, Arkansas and Texas and all the territories; the game must be played boldly"— *David Atchison, proslavery senator from Missouri.*

"I have only a short time to live—only one death to die, and I will die fighting for this cause. There will be no more peace in this land until slavery is done for."—*John Brown, abolitionist*

GLOSSARY

abolition
    The act of putting an end to.

border ruffian
    A proslavery Missourian who used violence and intimidation to skew the results of Kansas's territorial elections.

Bushwhacker
    A proslavery guerilla fighter from Missouri during the Civil War.

constitution
    A document stating the rules and establishing the structures by which a group of people, such as in a state or nation, will be governed.

emancipation
    The freeing of the slaves.

emigration
    Movement of settlers from one part of a country to another.

exoduster
    An African American from a former slave state in the South who participated in the exodus, or emigration, from the South to Kansas in the 1870s and 1880s.

free-stater
> An antislavery settler in the Kansas Territory in the Bleeding Kansas years; also called Free-Soiler.

guerilla
> An individual, often associated with a group, who engages in warfare independent of an army or government. They fight their enemies with sudden and surprise attacks.

impasse
> A deadlock.

indict
> To charge with an offense.

Jayhawker
> An antislavery guerilla fighter from Kansas and Missouri before and during the Civil War.

militia
> An army of citizens trained for emergencies and national defense.

popular sovereignty
> The view that voters within a territory should determine whether or not slavery would be permitted there.

ADDITIONAL RESOURCES

SELECTED BIBLIOGRAPHY

Etcheson, Nicole. *Bleeding Kansas: Contested Liberty in the Civil War Era*. Lawrence: UP of Kansas, 2004. Print.

Goodrich, Thomas. *War to the Knife: Bleeding Kansas, 1854–1861*. Mechanicsburg, PA: Stackpole, 1998. Print.

Miner, Craig. *Seeding Civil War: Kansas in the National News, 1854–1858*. Lawrence: UP of Kansas, 2008. Print.

Rawley, James A. *Race and Politics: "Bleeding Kansas" and the Coming of the Civil War*. Philadelphia, PA: Lippincott, 1969. Print.

FURTHER READINGS

Bjorklund, Ruth, and Trudi Strain Trueit. *Kansas*. New York: Marshall Cavendish Benchmark, 2009. Print.

Horn, Geoffrey M. *John Brown: Putting Action Above Words*. New York: Crabtree, 2010. Print.

Jordan, Anne Devereaux, and Virginia Schomp. *The Civil War*. New York: Marshall Cavendish Benchmark, 2007. Print.

Web Links

To learn more about Bleeding Kansas, visit ABDO Publishing Company online at **www.abdopublishing.com**. Web sites about Bleeding Kansas are featured on our Book Links page. These links are routinely monitored and updated to provide the most current information available.

Places to Visit

John Brown Museum
Tenth and Main Street, Osawatomie, Kansas 66064
913-755-4384
http://www.kshs.org/portal_john_brown
The museum was built around the Adair Cabin, the original home of John and Fiorella Adair, abolitionists and neighbors of Brown and his family in Osawatomie. It contains original furniture as well as pictures and exhibits about the Browns and the abolition movement.

Kansas Museum of History
6425 SW Sixth Ave., Topeka, KS 66615-1099
785-272-8681
http://www.kshs.org/portal_museum
Exhibits show the entire history of Kansas, including the Bleeding Kansas era and the Civil War.

Lawrence Visitor Center
402 N Second St., Lawrence, KS 66044
(756) 856-3040
http://www.visitlawrence.com/attractions/lawrence-visitor-center
The Lawrence Visitor Center, in the town's restored Union Pacific Depot, shows *Lawrence: Free State Fortress*, a free 25-minute docudrama about Lawrence's role in Bleeding Kansas and the Civil War. The center also provides free brochures.

Source Notes

Chapter 1. The Kansas Question
None.

Chapter 2. Slavery in the United States
1. "Quotations on Slavery and Emancipation." *Th. Jefferson Monticello*. Monticello.org, n.d. Web. 14 July 2011.
2. "Commitment to Purpose." *The Liberator Files*. Wordpress, 2011. Web. 14 July 2011.
3. William Lee Miller. *Arguing About Slavery: The Great Battle in the United States Congress*. New York: Knopf, 1996. Print. 37.
4. Randy Dotinga. "The Little Woman Behind a Very Big War." *Chapter & Verse*. The Christian Science Monitor, 30 June 2011. Web. 3 Aug. 2011.

Chapter 3. The Race to Kansas
1. John M. Murrin, Paul E. Johnson, James M. McPherson and Gary Gerstle. *Liberty, Equality, Power: A History of the American People*. Boston: Thomson Wadsworth. 2008. Print. 527.
2. Thomas Goodrich. *War to the Knife: Bleeding Kansas, 1854–1861*. Mechanicsburg, PA: Stackpole, 1998. Print. 10.
3. E. J. Fox. "Andrew H. Reeder." *Blue Skyways*. Tom & Carolyn Ward, 1998. Web. 14 July 2011.
4. Thomas Goodrich. *War to the Knife: Bleeding Kansas, 1854–1861*. Mechanicsburg, PA: Stackpole, 1998. Print.28.

Chapter 4. A Territory Divided
1. John Greenleaf Whittier. "The Conflict with Slavery, Politics and Reform, the Inner Life and Criticism." *The Works of Whittier, Volume VII*. Project Gutenberg, Dec. 2005. Web. 8 Aug. 2011.
2. David S. Reynolds. *John Brown, Abolitionist: The Man Who Killed Slavery, Sparked the Civil War, and Seeded Civil Rights*. New York: Knopf, 2005. Print. 146.
3. Thomas Goodrich. *War to the Knife: Bleeding Kansas, 1854–1861*. Mechanicsburg, PA: Stackpole, 1998. Print. 172.
4. Ibid. 85.

5. "Beecher Bibles." *Kansaspedia*. Kansas Historical Society, Dec. 2004. Web. 8 Aug. 2011.

6. Thomas Goodrich. *War to the Knife: Bleeding Kansas, 1854–1861*. Mechanicsburg, PA: Stackpole, 1998. Print.110.

7. "Kansas Herald of Freedom." *Lincoln at 200*. Newberry Library and Chicago History Museum, n.d. Web. 14 July 2011.

Chapter 5. Bleeding Kansas

1. Nicole Etcheson. *Bleeding Kansas: Contested Liberty in the Civil War Era*. Lawrence, KS: UP of Kansas, 2004. Print. 99.

2. Williamjames Hoffer. *The Caning of Charles Sumner: Honor, Idealism, and the Origins of the Civil War*. Baltimore, MD: Johns Hopkins UP, 2010. Print. 92.

3. Susan Welch, John Gruhl, John Comer, and Susan M. Rigdon. *Understanding American Government*. Boston: Wadsworth, Cengage Learning, 2010. Print. 278.

4. Ralph Waldo Emerson. *Emerson in His Journals*. Ed. Joel Porte. Cambridge, MA: Belknap, 1982. Print. 474.

5. David S. Reynolds. *John Brown, Abolitionist: The Man Who Killed Slavery, Sparked the Civil War, and Seeded Civil Rights*. New York: Knopf, 2005. Print. 202.

Chapter 6. The Path Toward Statehood

1. Russell K. Hickman. "The Early Years Concluded." *Kansas Historical Quarterly*. Kansas Historical Society, 2011. Web. 14 July 2011.

2. James Buchanan. *The Works of James Buchanan: Comprising His Speeches, State Papers, and Private Correspondence*. Ed. John Basset Moore. Philadelphia: J.B. Lippincott Company, 1910. Print. 97.

3. Robert Stone. "Kansas Laws and Their Origin." *Blue Skyways*. Tom & Carolyn Ward, 2000. Web. 8 Aug. 2011.

4. James W. Sheahan. *The Life of Stephen A. Douglas*. New York: Harper & Brothers, 1860. Print. 319.

SOURCE NOTES CONTINUED

Chapter 7. Guerilla Warfare
1. Thomas Goodrich. *War to the Knife: Bleeding Kansas, 1854–1861.* Mechanicsburg, PA: Stackpole, 1998. Print. 215.
2. Nicole Etcheson. *Bleeding Kansas: Contested Liberty in the Civil War Era.* Lawrence: UP of Kansas, 2004. Print. 186.
3. Ibid. 198.
4. David S. Reynolds. *John Brown, Abolitionist: The Man Who Killed Slavery, Sparked the Civil War, and Seeded Civil Rights.* New York: Knopf, 2005. Print. 282.
5. "James Redpath (1833–1891)." *American Experience.* PBS Online and WGBH, 1999. Web. 14 July 2011.

Chapter 8. Civil War
1. Nicole Etcheson. *Bleeding Kansas: Contested Liberty in the Civil War Era.* Lawrence: UP of Kansas, 2004. Print. 196.
2. Ibid. 224.
3. Christopher Phillips. "Missouri's War Within the War." *Opinionator.* The New York Times, 11 June 2011. Web. 8 Aug. 2011.
4. "THE ARMY AT SPRINGFIELD.; Great Change in the Aspect of Affairs A Battle Expected Soon Visit to the Wilson's Creek Battle-ground Zagonyi's Charge." *New York Times.* The New York Times, 11 Nov. 1861. Web. 8 Aug. 2011.
5. *Index to the Miscellaneous Documents of the House of Representatives for the Second Session of the Forty-Seventh Congress.* Washington: Government Printing Office, 1883. Print. 642.

Chapter 9. Bleeding Kansas Legacy

1. Craig Miner. *Seeding Civil War: Kansas in the National News, 1854–1858*. Lawrence: UP of Kansas, 2008. Print. 6.

2. "Richard M. Hoe." *Hall of Fame.* Invent Now, Inc, 2000–2011. Web. 8 Aug. 2011.

3. Harriet Beecher Stowe. "Sojourner Truth, The Libyan Sibyl." *Atlantic Monthly 11 (April 1863): 473–81*. Libraries of the U of Missouri-St. Louis, n.d. Web. 14 July 2011.

4. "Resolution for Kansas' Sesquicentennial." *CommunityNews.com*. News-Press & Gazette Company, NPG Newspapers, 2011. Web. 14 July 2011.

5. "Basic Readings in U.S. Democracy." *InfoUSA*. Bureau of International Information Programs, U.S. Department of State. n.d. Web. 25 July 2011.

INDEX

ABOUT THE AUTHOR

Richard Reece is a longtime writer and magazine editor. He has published magazine articles, poetry, and numerous works of fiction and nonfiction. A native of Kansas City, Missouri, with roots in Lawrence, Kansas, he currently resides in Raleigh, North Carolina, where he works as a magazine editor.

PHOTO CREDITS

North Wind Picture Archives/Alamy, cover, 3; North Wind Picture Archives/AP Images, 6, 14, 21, 33, 46, 82, 96 (top); MPI/Getty Images, 10, 45, 68, 76, 89, 97, 99; Popular Graphic Arts/Library of Congress, 13, 85; AP Images, 23, 28, 34, 55, 67; North Wind Picture Archives, 24, 59; Library of Congress, 36, 75, 91; Kean Collection/Getty Images, 51, 96 (bottom); N. Currier/Library of Congress, 56; Orlin Wagner/AP Images, 63, 98; Historic American Buildings Survey/Historic American Engineering Record/Library of Congress, 86; USPS/AP Images, 93; Walter G. Arce/Shutterstock Images, 95